Contents

Introduction

If you are wild about learning and wild about animals – this book is for you!

It will take you on a wild adventure, where you will practise key spelling skills and explore the amazing world of animals along the way.

Each spelling topic is introduced in a clear and simple way with lots of interesting activities to complete so that you can practise what you have learned. Don't forget that you can use your dictionary to help you!

Alongside every topic you will discover fascinating facts about the animals that live in the Australian outback. These animals thrive in the wide-open desert landscapes.

When you have completed each topic, record the animals that you have seen and the skills you have learned in the explorer's logbook on pages 44–45.

Good luck, explorer!

Shelley Welsh

Suffixes beginning with a vowel

A **suffix** is a letter or letter string added to the end of a **root word** (a word without a prefix or suffix) that changes or adds to its meaning. For some one-syllable words, just add the suffix.

dart + ing = dart__ing__   trick + ed = trick__ed__

For others, the final consonant needs to be doubled before adding the suffix.

tap + ing = tap__ping__   shop + ing = shop__ping__

Say the two-syllable words' forget' and 'begin' out loud. The last syllable is stressed. For words of more then one syllable where the last syllable is stressed, double the final consonant.

forget + ing = forge__tting__   begin + ing = begin__ning__

However, if the last syllable is *not* stressed, the final consonant is not doubled.

garden + ing = garde__ning__   garden + er = garde__ner__

Task 1	Add the suffixes **ing** and **ed** to these words.

a park _____ _____

b pick _____ _____

c track _____ _____

d sort _____ _____

Task 2
Add the suffixes **ing** and **ed** to these words.

	ing	ed
open		
trumpet		
fidget		
limit		

WILD FACT
Female kangaroos have pouches containing mammary glands, where they keep their young until they are old enough.

Task 3
Add a suitable suffix from the box to complete the words below.

| ed   ing   en |

a The enthusiastic explorers were **forbid** _____ from taking photographs of the kangaroos.

b The World Wildlife Fund said they were **commit** _____ to protecting kangaroos in the wild.

c A boxing match **occur** _____ between two male kangaroos.

d We are already **regret** _____ not spending longer in the outback with the roos.

WILD FACT
A group of kangaroos is called a mob, a herd or a troop. To alert others to danger, they stamp their strong back feet on the ground.

Exploring Further ...

Unscramble the words below and then add the suffixes **ing** and **ed**.

	word	ing	ed
a	itmad		
b	wasren		
c	premit		

Now hop to pages 44–45 to record what you have learned in your explorer's logbook.

3

The suffix ation

The suffix **ation** can be added to some **verbs** to form **nouns**.

inform + ation = information

Sometimes you might need to make changes to the spelling. If the verb ends in **e**, delete it before you add the suffix **ation**.

adore + ation = adoration

Other words behave differently. You will just have to learn them!

pronounce + ation = pronunciation

multiply + ation = multiplication

FACT FILE

Animal: Wallaby
Habitat: Shrub, brush and rocky areas
Weight: 2 to 24 kg
Lifespan: Up to 9 years
Diet: Grasses and plants

WILD FACT

The wallaby uses its powerful back legs to hop about. Young wallabies are known as 'joeys', like young koalas.

Task 1	Add **ation** to these verbs to form a noun.

a form _____

b consider _____

c plant _____

d confirm _____

e confront _____

Task 2 Change the verb in the brackets to make a noun that completes each sentence.

a The explorers decided there should be a _____ of their wallaby research. (**continue**)

b When I said the wallaby I rescued weighed 30 kg, it was not an _____. (**exaggerate**)

c The outback vet said an _____ was needed before setting the wallaby free. (**examine**)

d The researcher's _____ of a wallaby fact file was welcomed. (**create**)

Task 3 Choose an appropriate verb from the box and turn it into a noun to complete the sentences.

> **tempt illustrate prepare exclaim fascinate**

a My brother had a _____ for wallabies.

b The _____ for our outback trip was very thorough.

c The _____ to stay longer in Australia was on our minds.

d I drew a quick _____ of the wallaby before it disappeared.

e "Wow!" was my immediate _____ when the wallaby hopped off.

WILD FACT

The wallaby's tail is as long as its body. It uses it to fend off predators.

Exploring Further ...

Add the suffix **ation** to the verbs on the left to fill in the table with correctly spelt nouns.

communicate	ation	
transport	ation	
register	ation	
locate	ation	

Now leap to pages 44–45 to record what you have learned in your explorer's logbook.

The suffix *ly*

Animal:	Koala
Habitat:	Eastern Australia, in eucalyptus trees
Weight:	Up to 13 kg
Lifespan:	Up to 20 years
Diet:	Eucalyptus leaves

The suffix **ly** can be added to an **adjective** to form an **adverb**. If the root word ends in **e**, the **e** is usually deleted and replaced with **ly**.

sad + ly = sadly   true + ly = truly

There are exceptions to this rule!

polite + ly = politely   fine + ly = finely

If the root word ends in **y** with a consonant before it, the **y** is changed to **i** as long as the root word has more than one syllable.

happy + ly = happily

If the root word ends in **le**, the **le** changes to **ly**.

gentle + ly = gently

If the root word ends in **ic**, the suffix **ally** is added.

comic + ly = comically

There is an exception to this rule!

public ⟶ publicly

WILD FACT

Babies, born blind with no hair and no ears, spend their first few months in their mother's pouch and are known as 'joeys'.

Task 1 Add **ly** to the following adjectives to form adverbs.

Adjective	Adverb
calm	
nice	
sweet	
pleasant	
brave	

Task 2 Write the correct spelling of each underlined adverb on the line.

a We are <u>terribley</u> upset to be leaving the outback. _____

b The trip has been <u>simpley</u> fantastic. _____

c Although we are <u>basicaly</u> exhausted, we would like to stay. _____

d The koalas will be <u>franticaly</u> looking for us! _____

Task 3 Rewrite these sentences so that they contain adverbs formed from the adjectives in the box.

happy   angry   hungry   lazy

a I was skipping through the outback.

_____

b The koala bear lay on the branch.

_____

c The koala bear ate the eucalyptus leaves.

_____

d The carpet snake hissed at the explorer.

_____

Exploring Further ...

Turn the adjectives into adverbs and use them to write sentences. Extra witchetty grubs if they are about koalas!

Adjective	Sentence
enthusiastic	
comical	
nimble	

Now climb to pages 44–45 to record what you have learned in your explorer's logbook.

Prefixes un, in, im, ir and il

A **prefix** is a group of letters added to the beginning of a word to turn it into another word. Usually there are no changes in spelling. The prefixes can have a negative meaning: 'not'.

kind ⟶ <u>un</u>kind

correct ⟶ <u>in</u>correct

If the root word starts with the letter **l**, the prefix **il** is used instead of **in**.

legal ⟶ <u>il</u>legal

If the root word starts with the letter **m** or **p**, the prefix **im** is used instead of **in**.

possible ⟶ <u>im</u>possible

If the root word starts with the letter **r**, the prefix **ir** is used instead of **in**.

responsible ⟶ <u>ir</u>responsible

Task 1	Add the correct prefix of **un** or **in** to these words.

a happy _____

b accurate _____

c stable _____

d active _____

e decent _____

FACT FILE

Animal: Brushtail possum

Habitat: Forests and urban areas

Weight: 1.2 to 4.5 kg

Lifespan: Up to 13 years

Diet: Eucalyptus leaves

Task 2   Add either the prefix **ir** or **in** to the words in brackets to complete the sentences.

a The newborn possum had an _____ heartbeat. (**regular**)

b My fear of the possum was completely _____. (**rational**)

c We were _____ of capturing the possum. (**capable**)

d People who don't live in Australia think urban possums are _____. (**offensive**)

e Don't be _____ by leaving food out for pesky possums. (**responsible**)

Task 3   Unravel the anagrams to find words starting with the prefixes **il** or **im**.

a il teriatel   _____

b im sonpreal   _____

c im morla   _____

d il galel   _____

WILD FACT

The brushtail possum is well-known as a nocturnal pest that forages in bins and raids garden fruit trees. Although it is a herbivore, it has been known to eat small mammals.

Exploring Further ...

Match the prefixes below to the correct root word – make sure every possum is fed!

un

in

ir

il

adequate

necessary

legible

responsible

WILD FACT

The brushtail possum has a bushy tail that is adapted to grasping branches. Smelly secretions from its pouch keep predators away.

Now leap to pages **44–45** to record what you have learned in your explorer's logbook.

Prefixes *dis* and *mis*

WILD FACT

When naturalists first saw pictures of the platypus, they thought it was a hoax because it looked so odd!

The prefixes **dis** and **mis** usually give the root word a **negative** or **opposite** meaning.

obey ⟶ *disobey*
interpret ⟶ *misinterpret*

There are no rules about these prefixes: you just have to learn them!

FACT FILE

Animal: Platypus
Habitat: Freshwater lakes and streams; burrows above water level
Weight: Up to 1.4 kg
Lifespan: Up to 17 years
Diet: Insects, larvae, shellfish and worms

Task 1 Add either the prefix **dis** or **mis** to these words.

a appoint _____

b understand _____

c honest _____

d connect _____

e fortune _____

Task 2   Add either **dis** or **mis** to the following words to complete the sentences below.

(agree)   (similar)   (advantage)   (heard)

a The platypus's bill is not _____ to a duck's.

b I wouldn't _____ that the platypus is an unusual-looking mammal.

c When the platypus gave a low-pitched growl, I thought I'd _____.

d On land, the platypus is at a _____ due to its short, heavy legs.

Task 3   Write down the words that start with the prefix **dis** or **mis** that these definitions are describing.

a Not faithful or loyal: _____

b Spell incorrectly: _____

c Not honourable: _____

d Not connected: _____

e Bad luck: _____

WILD FACT

The platypus has a tail like a beaver, a bill like a duck, feet like an otter and it lays eggs! The male even has a venomous spur on its back foot. If disturbed, they will utter a low growl.

Exploring Further …

Circle eight words in the word-search that start with the prefixes **mis** or **dis**.

R	A	N	C	D	B	X	N	D	E
D	A	L	W	W	Q	E	Y	I	V
A	I	E	W	A	K	F	D	S	A
E	U	V	P	A	C	I	E	C	H
L	P	T	T	P	S	Q	Y	O	E
S	H	S	S	T	A	W	D	V	B
I	I	I	R	G	U	S	A	E	S
M	U	U	U	Q	I	O	I	R	I
M	S	Y	E	B	O	S	I	D	M
T	M	M	I	S	P	L	A	C	E

Now burrow to pages 44–45 to record what you have learned in your explorer's logbook.

Prefixes re, sub and inter

The prefix **re** means 'again' or 'back'.

re + turn = return

The prefix **sub** means 'under'.

sub + marine = submarine

The prefix **inter** means 'between' or 'among'.

inter + active = interactive

WILD FACT

Echidnas have short, strong limbs with large claws. They feed by tearing open soft logs and anthills, using their long, sticky tongue to capture their prey. They have tiny mouths and toothless jaws.

Task 1 Add the suffix **re** to the following root words, then write a definition for each new word.

a appear _____

_____

b decorate _____

_____

c discover _____

_____

d do _____

_____

Task 2 — Match the word to the correct definition.

a subscribe   an underground walkway

b subheading   to arrange to receive something, e.g. a magazine

c subtitle   translation of foreign language on screen

d subway   a heading given to a section of writing

WILD FACT

Echidnas are the planet's oldest surviving mammals. They can survive extremes of temperatures with some species adapting to cold by growing fur, rather than spines.

Task 3 — Insert an appropriate word from the box to complete these sentences, about echidnas.

| researchers   intermingle   interchangeable   resubmit |

a The name 'echidna' is _____ with 'spiny anteater'.

b _____ discovered that male echidnas have non-venomous spurs on their hind feet.

c Because the explorers got some of their facts wrong, they had to _____ their report.

d They are solitary creatures that do not like to _____.

Exploring Further …

Match these root words to the correct prefix.
Hint: Some words may go with more than one prefix!

send   **sub**   merge

national   **inter**   act

heading   **re**   fresh

Now rustle your way to pages 44–45 to record what you have learned in your explorer's logbook.

Prefixes super, anti and auto

The prefix **super** means 'above' or 'beyond'.

super + market = <u>super</u>market

The prefix **anti** means 'against' or 'opposed to'.

anti + septic = <u>anti</u>septic

The prefix **auto** means 'self'.

auto + biography = <u>auto</u>biography

FACT FILE

Animal:	Cassowary
Habitat:	Palm scrub, grassland, savannah and swamp forest
Weight:	Up to 58 kg
Lifespan:	40 to 50 years
Diet:	Fruit, seeds, snails, insects, frogs and birds

Task 1 Write a definition for the following words starting with the prefix 'super'.

a superhuman _____

b supermarket _____

c superstar _____

d supermodel _____

Task 2

Insert a word from the box into the correct sentence below.

| anticlockwise | antisocial | antibiotic |

a The research laboratory developed an _____ to protect cassowaries against disease.

b We followed the cassowary through the rainforest in an _____ direction.

c Working for days on end in an outback research centre might seem _____ to some.

WILD FACT

Cassowaries are vital for seed dispersal in Australia's rainforests. However, they are under threat of extinction due to habitat loss, road deaths and attacks by dogs.

Task 3

Match the words below with the correct definition. Draw a trail of cassowary prints – 人 片 – to link the two!

a autograph   extra-large shop

b autopilot   active against bacteria

c superstore   your own signature

d antibacterial   automatic steering device

WILD FACT

The name *cassowary* comes from two Papuan words: 'kasu' meaning 'horned' and 'weri' meaning 'head', referring to the 'helmet' on its head.

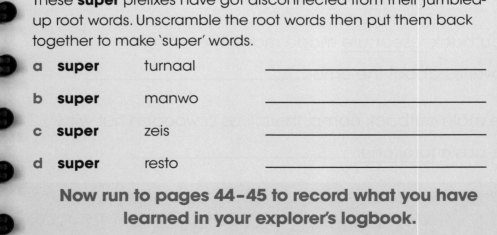

Exploring Further ...

These **super** prefixes have got disconnected from their jumbled-up root words. Unscramble the root words then put them back together to make 'super' words.

a **super** turnaal _____

b **super** manwo _____

c **super** zeis _____

d **super** resto _____

Now run to pages 44–45 to record what you have learned in your explorer's logbook.

Words ending sure and ture

It's quite easy to tell the difference between words ending in **sure** and **ture**. Say these words **out loud**:

trea<u>sure</u>   *adven<u>ture</u>*

Some words sound like they might end in **ture** but actually end in **cher**:

tea<u>cher</u>   *stret<u>cher</u>*

FACT FILE

Animal: Emu
Habitat: Forest and savannah woodland
Weight: Up to 60 kg
Lifespan: 10 to 20 years
Diet: Plants, grasshoppers, crickets and ladybirds

Task 1   Write the correct spelling of the underlined words on the answer lines.

a   Joe loved being an explorer because he was very in touch with <u>natcher</u>. _____

b   The outback <u>researture</u> made many interesting discoveries about the emu. _____

c   In the main outback camp, there was a wooden hut with some basic <u>furnitcher</u>. _____

Task 2

Unravel the anagrams below that spell words ending in **sure** and **ture**. The first letter of each word is in red.

a ru**e**vent _____

b ru**s**elea**p** _____

c ru**t**erea**c** _____

d rus**e**cloen _____

e tric**e**u**ps** _____

Task 3

Complete the short story below using an appropriate word from Task 2. Some words may change from singular to plural.

The explorers were feeling apprehensive about their next _____ into the outback. However, they were very excited about seeing a range of interesting _____. Each explorer had a camera with them to take _____ of cassowaries, echidnas and kangaroos. The expedition leader said she would put a crocodile in a temporary _____ so they could take photographs safely. In the end, all the explorers agreed what a _____ it had been.

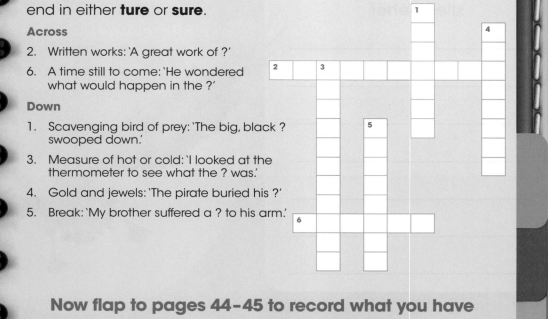

Exploring Further ...

All the answers in the crossword end in either **ture** or **sure**.

Across

2. Written works: 'A great work of ?'
6. A time still to come: 'He wondered what would happen in the ?'

Down

1. Scavenging bird of prey: 'The big, black ? swooped down.'
3. Measure of hot or cold: 'I looked at the thermometer to see what the ? was.'
4. Gold and jewels: 'The pirate buried his ?'
5. Break: 'My brother suffered a ? to his arm.'

Now flap to pages 44–45 to record what you have learned in your explorer's logbook.

Silent letters

Some letters that were **sounded** in words hundreds of years ago are no longer sounded today. The letters often remain in the spellings, however. For example, 'knight' used to be pronounced with a hard 'k' sound.

knit   know   comb   numb

Task 1

Write seven words that start with a silent letter.

a _____

b _____

c _____

d _____

e _____

f _____

g _____

Task 2 Underline the silent letters in these words.

comb

gnarl

sword

Wednesday

honest

island

Task 3 Underline the silent letter in each word in the box, then use the words to complete the sentences below.

| knowledge sign wrack doubt knew |

a There is no _____ that the Australian pelican is an impressive water bird.

b I _____ it had a long bill but I didn't know it was the longest of any bird in the world!

c I had to _____ my brains to think of other birds with long bills.

d However, I clearly need to improve my _____ of birds as I couldn't think of any.

e This is a clear _____ that I need to do a bit more research.

Exploring Further ...

Complete the words below with their missing letters, one of which is a silent letter. To help you, the silent letters are given to you in red.

(g) d __ si __ n   f __ rei __ __   __ n __ me

(b) cr __ m __   b __ m __   th __ m __

(n) a __ tum __   c __ lum __   h __ m __

(t) f __ s __ en   ca __ __ l __   wh __ s __ l __

Now float to pages 44–45 to record what you have learned in your explorer's logbook.

Words ending ous

If the root word ends in a **consonant**, then add the suffix **ous** in the normal way.

poison → poison<u>ous</u>

If it ends in a vowel, take the vowel off.

fame → fam<u>ous</u>

If it ends in a **y**, then the **y** becomes **i**.

vary → var<u>ious</u>

However, if the root word ends in a soft 'g' sound followed by **e**, then the **e** stays.

courage → courag<u>eous</u>

If the root word ends in **our**, then it changes to **or** before the suffix **ous** is added.

humour → hum<u>orous</u>

FACT FILE

Animal: Fruit bat
Habitat: Trees
Weight: 907 g
Lifespan: 20 to 30 years
Diet: Mangos, dates, avocados and other fruit

Task 1

Add **ous** to the following words to make adjectives.

a danger _____

b mountain _____

c fame _____

d outrage _____

e ridicule _____

f envy _____

WILD FACT

Fruit bats have the nickname 'flying foxes' – their foxy faces are a clue as to why! They have big eyes, small ears and a long nose.

Use a dictionary to help you join the words in the bats to their correct definitions.

a **vigorous** extremely large

b **glamorous** envious

c **jealous** strong and healthy

d **enormous** stylish and fashionable

WILD FACT

Fruit bats are the only mammals that can fly. They hang upside down in trees, not caves, and some species wrap their wings round their bodies to keep warm!

Task 3 Complete the sentences in this short passage with an appropriate word from the box.

tremendous poisonous famous various

Steve Irwin was a _____ Australian crocodile hunter. He presented

_____ television documentaries about Australian outback animals.

Sadly he died after being stabbed by a stingray with its _____ barb.

Throughout his life he showed that he was a _____ animal expert.

Exploring Further ...

Find the 10 words ending in **ous** in this word-search. The first letter of each word is marked in red.

S	N	X	S	S	C	D	S	Q	T	D	K
H	T	K	U	U	O	H	U	X	R	W	V
V	R	O	O	O	U	I	O	X	E	S	H
T	P	M	I	M	R	L	I	Y	M	U	Y
T	E	T	R	R	A	A	V	B	E	O	V
O	U	L	U	O	G	R	B	J	N	R	G
D	M	J	C	N	E	I	O	S	D	T	E
U	R	P	D	E	O	O	Z	U	O	S	X
W	V	R	S	T	U	U	Q	O	U	A	L
E	I	D	H	T	S	S	O	M	S	S	S
S	U	O	L	A	E	J	A	A	O	I	N
S	U	O	I	R	E	S	F	F	U	D	S

Now flap to pages 44–45 to record what you have learned in your explorer's logbook.

Words with an *ay* sound

Not all words are spelt as they are pronounced. Look at these words that have an 'ay' sound, but are spelled with **ei**, **eigh** or **ey**.

beige   eight   they

Task 1

Unravel these anagrams to reveal words with an **ei** spelling. The first letter of each word is in red.

a ge**t**whi _____

b **n**iev _____

c bour**n**ighe _____

d **r**igen _____

e d**r**iwe _____

f geei**b** _____

g thyi**e**g _____

h **r**ehi _____

FACT FILE

Animal: Jacana
Habitat: Freshwater wetlands
Weight: 150 to 260 g
Lifespan: Up to 5 years
Diet: Seeds and aquatic insects

Task 2   Underline the correctly spelt word in the brackets in these sentences.

a The comb-crested jacana (**ways/weighs**) 150–260 kg.

b (**They/thay**) stand on water lilies while looking for insects to eat.

c My (**neighbour/neybour**) is an explorer.

d She will be visiting (**ate/eight**) different states and territories in Australia.

e Her exploration involves conducting a (**survay/survey**) on jacanas.

Task 3   The following underlined words have been spelt as they sound and they are all incorrect! Write the correct spelling on the answer line provided.

a The bird of <u>pray</u> attacked the comb-crested jacana.   _____

b I saw a comb-crested jacana with a <u>bage</u> wing-tip.   _____

c In the Blue Mountains we went on a <u>slay</u>.   _____

d We wouldn't <u>disobay</u> our outback expedition guide.   _____

Exploring Further ...

The missing words in these sentences have an 'ay' sound but either an **ei**, **eigh** or **ey** spelling. What could they be? The first letter of each word is provided to give you a clue.

a   Nineteenth-century female explorers wore <u>v_____</u> over their faces to protect them from insects in the outback.

b   Native aborigines carried tents and supplies and did not dare <u>d_____</u> the European men in charge.

c   It was a hard job because of the heavy <u>w_____</u> of the equipment and the extreme heat.

d   Expedition members wore camouflage green, brown and <u>b_____</u> outfits.

Now pick your way to pages 44–45 to record what you have learned in your explorer's logbook.

Apostrophes for possession

FACT FILE

Animal: Laughing kookaburra
Habitat: Humid forests and arid savannahs
Weight: Up to 465 g
Lifespan: 11 to 12 years
Diet: Mice, insects, lizards, snakes and small birds

We use an **apostrophe** to show **possession**.

The girl's shoes.

When the noun is plural, the apostrophe goes after the final **s**.

The babies' rattles.

If the plural noun does not end in **s**, then an apostrophe followed by **s** is added.

The children's games.

Places and people's names ending in **s** usually end with an apostrophe followed by **s**.

Charles's new laptop.

Task 1 Add an apostrophe and an **s** to these singular nouns to show possession.

a The **crocodile** _____ teeth.

b The **pelican** _____ feet.

c The **bat** _____ wing span.

d The **camel** _____ hump.

e The **snake** _____ venom.

f The **kangaroo** _____ pouch.

WILD FACT

The call of the kookaburra sounds like it is laughing. Females nest in holes in trees and lay between one and five eggs, with their mate and siblings staying close by to help care for them.

Task 2

Add an apostrophe to these plural nouns to show possession, then put one into each sentence below.

| dingoes kookaburras koalas platypuses |

a The _____ calls sounded like they were laughing.

b The _____ pups were really sweet!

c The _____ noses were black and shiny.

d The _____ bills make them look a bit like ducks.

Task 3

The proper nouns at the start of these sentences need an apostrophe and an s to show possession.

a Chris _____ study of the laughing kookaburra made an interesting report.

b Australia _____ outback is full of interesting animals.

c Cairns _____ mangrove areas contain the deadly box jellyfish.

WILD FACT

Kookaburras anger farmers by preying on chickens. Due to the early morning cackling chorus of the kookaburra, they have earned the nickname 'bushman's clock'.

Exploring Further ...

The apostrophes in the following sentences are either missing or in the wrong place. Rewrite each sentence correctly on the lines below.

a My friends map was found covered in muddy paw print's.

_____

_____

b All the explorers's sunhats were stolen by some cheeky koala bears'.

_____

_____

c The small expeditions' final camp was close to the billabong's.

_____

_____

Now laugh all the way to pages 44–45 to record what you have learned in your explorer's logbook.

Homophones and near-homophones

Homophones are words that sound the same or very similar but have different spellings (usually), and different meanings.

Look at these two words.

hair   hare

Some homophones are tricky because even though they don't sound the same, they sound similar enough that people often misspell them. They are called **near-homophones**.

affect   effect

FACT FILE

Animal:	Carpet snake
Habitat:	Rainforests, arid and coastal regions
Weight:	Up to 15 kg
Lifespan:	Up to 20 years
Diet:	Mammals, birds and lizards

Task 1 Write a homophone for the following words.

a right   _____

b seen   _____

c weather   _____

d not   _____

e here   _____

f meet   _____

WILD FACT

Carpet snakes are quite harmless despite the fact that they can grow up to 3.5 metres in length. They are great rat catchers!

Task 2

There is something wrong with the underlined words in these sentences. Rewrite each sentence below, using the correct word.

a   The carpet snake kills by constricting its <u>pray</u>.

_____

b   The laughing kookaburra nests in <u>wholes</u> in trees.

_____

c   My friend, <u>who's</u> dinner was eaten by a possum, was starving.

_____

Task 3

Create two short sentences for each pair of words to show the difference in their meanings.

a   lead   led

_____

_____

b   passed   past

_____

_____

WILD FACT

The carpet snake is a blotchy olive-green, brown and beige in colour, which provides good camouflage. It tends to be active at night and during the day enjoys coiling itself around a branch.

Exploring Further ...

Draw a carpet snake around the correct near-homophones below.

a   The explorers **wondered** / **wandered** into the outback.

b   It was time to **accept** / **except** that we had to leave the outback.

c   A snake expert was the **guest** / **guessed** speaker.

Now slither to pages 44–45 to record what you have learned in your explorer's logbook.

27

k and sh sounds spelt ch

Some words – usually ones that come from Greek – have a 'k' sound that is spelt **ch**.

character

Other words, most of which come from French, have a 'sh' sound that is spelt **ch**.

chalet

FACT FILE

Animal: Desert death adder
Habitat: Remote areas, amongst porcupine grass and stony flats
Size: Up to 70 cm
Lifespan: 15 to 20 years in the wild
Diet: Lizards, birds, snakes and dragonflies

Task 1 Underline the 'k' sounds in these words and then insert them into the sentences below.

mechanic   ache   school   stomachs

a After being nipped by the cassowary, I had a bit of an _____.

b At _____ we learned all about Australian outback animals.

c Camels have three _____ in their digestive system.

d We needed a _____ to fix our expedition's four-wheel drive.

Task 2 These words have been spelt incorrectly. Write the correct spelling on the line beside each one.

a karacter _____

b kemist _____

c korus _____

d eko _____

WILD FACT

Unlike most other snakes, desert death adders don't lay eggs but give birth to live young. As many as 15 to 20 may be produced in one litter.

Task 3 Untangle these anagrams that contain the letter string **ch**, but are pronounced either **k** or **sh**. The first letter of each word is in red.

a chupearat _____

b rachittec _____

c chemes _____

d chorna _____

WILD FACT

The desert death adder is one of the most dangerous snakes of all. It is red, orange and yellow in colour with a short, thick body, triangular head and a tapered, thin tail. Its tail tip, which is darker than the rest of its body, is used to attract potential prey.

Exploring Further ...

Fill in the missing letters in the words below then, using them all, write a short murder-mystery story starring the celebrated detective, Doctor Desmond D'Eath-Adder . . .

a ___ef

b ___auffeur

c ma___ine

d mousta___e

_____

_____

_____

_____

_____

Now slither to pages 44–45 to record what you have learned in your explorer's logbook.

Words with the s sound spelt sc

Some words that come from Latin have a 's' sound spelt **sc**.

scene

It may sound odd, but the Romans probably pronounced the **s** and the **k** as two sounds, rather than one.

s-k-een

WILD FACT

'Salties', as saltwater crocodiles are known in Australia, have been known to eat wild pigs, buffaloes and livestock such as cattle and horses. Some males have been recorded as measuring 6m to 7m.

Task 1

Use a dictionary to help you match these **sc** words to their correct definitions.

a	ascend	a follower of a leader
b	crescent	to move downwards
c	disciple	curved, sickle-shaped
d	descend	to move upwards

FACT FILE

Animal: The estuarine or saltwater crocodile

Habitat: Brackish water on the coast but also rivers, swamps and billabongs

Weight: Up to 1000kg

Lifespan: 70 years

Diet: Reptiles, fish, turtles and wading birds

Task 2 Insert the words from Task 1 into the sentences below. You will need to change the spelling of some of the words so that they make sense.

a Our expedition leader joked that we were great _____ who had learned a lot.

b As we made our final _____ of Ayers Rock, we got a great view of Uluru-Kata Tjuta National Park.

c It was evening, and there was a pale _____ moon in the sky above us.

d Once we had _____, we lit the camp fire and sang songs under the stars.

Task 3 Fill in the missing letters in these words.

a fluore __ __ ent

b mi __ __ ellaneous

c resu __ __ itate

d __ __ ent

e adole __ __ ent

f de __ __ end

WILD FACT

The saltwater crocodile is the largest of all reptiles. It is the most dangerous animal in Australia, killing on average one to two people per year.

Exploring Further ...

Write your own sentences containing the following words.

| science | fascinate | isosceles | scissors |

_____

_____

_____

_____

Now hunt your way to pages 44–45 to record what you have learned in your explorer's logbook.

g sound *gue*
and *k*
sound *que*

Some words, which come from French, end with a hard 'g' sound spelt **gue**.

league

Others words, also from French, end with a 'k' sound and are spelt **que**.

unique

FACT FILE

Animal: Freshwater or Johnson crocodile

Habitat: Swamps, billabongs and lagoons

Weight: Up to 100 kg

Lifespan: Up to 50 years

Diet: Fish, insects, small invertebrates, amphibians, mammals and birds

---

Task 1 Use the words in the crocodile to complete these sentences.

league   colleague   analogue   synagogue

a I prefer my _____ watch to my sister's digital one.

b As part of our religious education trip, we visited the local _____.

c My dad's _____ invited him to play golf.

d Our team was top of the football _____.

Task 2   Read the passage below, then rewrite the underlined words spelt correctly.

After walking in the outback, we all felt great <u>fateeg</u>. Our <u>tongs</u> were sticking to the roofs of our mouths. I heard a <u>dialog</u> between the leader and the guides. They'd seen a <u>roge</u> crocodile close to our camp.

_____   _____

_____   _____

Task 3   Put these words in a sentence, using a dictionary to check their meaning.

a boutique

_____

b opaque

_____

c picturesque

_____

Exploring Further ...

Find nine words ending in **gue** and **que** in this word-search.

M	O	E	R	M	F	F	E	C	E
O	O	R	U	Z	G	U	O	L	U
N	J	P	C	G	Q	X	D	I	G
O	B	R	A	I	N	I	X	Q	I
L	O	C	T	Q	A	I	W	U	T
O	R	N	I	L	U	V	R	E	A
G	A	S	O	G	J	E	N	E	F
U	S	G	D	E	Y	Y	G	S	M
E	U	G	O	L	O	R	P	B	U
E	T	O	N	G	U	E	M	B	Z

Now snap to pages 44–45 to record what you have learned in your explorer's logbook.

Letter strings *ou* and *ough*

Some words with an 'uh' sound are spelt with the letter string **ou**.

touch

You just need to learn them!

Other words have an 'uf' sound and are spelt with the letter string **ough**.

enough

FACT FILE

Animal:	Camel
Habitat:	Northern Territory desert and outback areas
Weight:	Up to 640 kg
Lifespan:	40 to 50 years
Diet:	Plants and grasses

Task 1 Unscramble the **ou** words in bold in these sentences then write them on the lines.

a Camels can be found not just in Australia but in many other **triesnouc** too.

_____

b Dromedaries have one hump, but Bactrian camels have a **oubled** hump.

_____

c Camels grazing in the Northern Territory cause **loubtre** by eating food harvested by Aborigines.

_____

Task 2

Write the **ou** words that these definitions are describing. The first letter of each word has been given to help you.

a Not old
y _____

b The child of a parent's sister or brother
c _____

c To cheer on, motivate
e _____

d Two together
c _____

WILD FACT

Camels have three stomachs for digesting their food multiple times. Their eyelashes are very long to keep sand and dust out of their eyes, and they have thick lips for protection when eating spiky plants.

Task 3

The words in bold in these sentences have been spelt as they sound. Write the correct spelling on the line below.

a It was **tuff** following the herd of camels for three days.

_____

b We slept on **ruff** ground at night to save carrying our camp beds.

_____

c There weren't **enuf** trees for shade, so we often woke in bright sunshine.

_____

d It took **cuhrage** for me to climb onto the camel's back.

_____

Exploring Further ...

Complete the crossword with 'ou' or 'ough' words

Across

2. Two of something

4. Food you need for growth and health

6. Bravery

Down

1. Land mass

3. Feel

5. Opposite of smooth

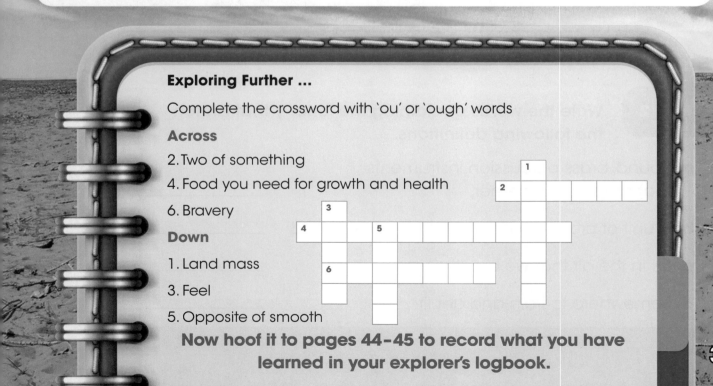

Now hoof it to pages 44–45 to record what you have learned in your explorer's logbook.

Tricky spellings

There are some tricky spellings in English! Some words have an 'i' sound spelt with a **y** in the middle of the word.

myth

Some words that end in **le** and **al** have a similar end sound.

possible

occasional

Task 1 Write the correct spelling of the following words.

a simbol _____

b Egipt _____

c piramid _____

d mistery _____

e himn _____

WILD FACT

Water buffalo live in swampy areas. They have backward-curving horns and a grey skin at birth, which turns slate-blue later.

FACT FILE

Animal: Water buffalo
Habitat: Marshes and billabongs
Weight: 300 to 550 kg
Lifespan: Up to 25 years
Diet: Reeds and marsh grasses

Task 2 Write the words containing the letter **y** that match the following definitions.

a Round, brass percussion instruments that are struck together. _____

b A unit of pronunciation with one vowel sound. _____

c It's in the air that we breathe. _____

d Somewhere to train and get fit. _____

Task 3 Add **al** or **le** to the words in the box, then insert them into the sentences.

| origin   ank   probab   addition   beet |

a After we saw a herd of water buffalo, we made an _____ discovery.

b The cave we found was full of _____ aboriginal drawings.

c It's quite _____ that they had been there for at least 100 years.

d We shared our shelter with a glossy rhino _____ with large horns.

e He felt tickly as he ran over my _____.

WILD FACT

There has been some cross-breeding between water buffalo and river buffalo, and some of these crossbreeds are used for milk production. Their milk is richer in fat and protein than a dairy cow's.

Exploring Further ...

Underline the correctly spelt word in each pair of words.

a The **capital/capitle** of Australia is Canberra.

b Some Aborigines still rely on very **practicle/practical** cooking methods.

c It's **possible/possibal** for water buffalo to live for 25 years.

d It was quite a **spectacal/spectacle** to see so many buffalo.

Now wallow to pages 44–45 to record what you have learned in your explorer's logbook.

Endings sounding like *shun*

Many words end in **tion**, **sion**, **ssion** and **cian** but they all sound the same! This can make spelling tricky.

The most common suffix is **tion** which is used if the root word ends in **t** or **te**. Remember to take off the **e** before you add the suffix.

hesitate ——→ *hesita<u>tion</u>*   *invent* ——→ *inven<u>tion</u>*

Use **ssion** if the root word ends in **ss** or **mit**. Remember to take off the **t** from **mit** before you add the suffix.

express ——→ *expre<u>ssion</u>*   *admit* ——→ *admi<u>ssion</u>*

Use **sion** if the root word ends in **d** or **se**. Remember to take off the **d** and **e** before you add the suffix.

expand ——→ *expan<u>sion</u>*   *tense* ——→ *ten<u>sion</u>*

Use **cian** if the root word ends in **c** or **cs**.

music ——→ *musi<u>cian</u>*   *mathematics* ——→ *mathemati<u>cian</u>*

FACT FILE

Animal: Dingo
Habitat: Throughout the mainland, close to a water source
Weight: From 13 kg to 20 kg
Lifespan: Up to 10 years
Diet: Rodents, birds and lizards

Task 1   Add the suffix **tion** to the following words.

a act   _____

b complete   _____

c inject   _____

d interrupt   _____

e coordinate   _____

Task 2   Write the correct word on the line by adding the suffix **sion** or **ssion** to the verbs in brackets.

a The startled (**express**) on the dingo's face was comical! _____

b He had no (**comprehend**) about where we could have come from.

_____

c You could see the (**tense**) in his muscles.

_____

d We asked our expedition leader for (**permit**) to go a little closer.

_____

Task 3   Add the suffix **cian** to these words to make nouns.

a electric   _____

b magic   _____

c music   _____

d optic   _____

Exploring Further ...

Unravel these anagrams, then use either the suffix **sion**, **ssion**, **tion** or **cian** to change them into another word. The dingo pawprint tells you which letter each word starts with.

a col(p)itis   _____   _____

b dext(e)n   _____   _____

c sosess(p)   _____   _____

d (c)opmleet   _____   _____

Now trot to pages 44–45 to record what you have learned in your explorer's logbook.

Dictionary work

Dictionaries tell us much more than just the meaning of words. They can tell us:

- how to **pronounce** the word, by separating the syllables and which syllable(s) to stress

- the **plural** of the word if it is a noun

- the word's **origin**, where relevant

- the word **type** – noun (n.), adjective (adj.), adverb (adv.), verb (v.) etc

- **synonyms** for the word (a synonym is a word that means the same or nearly the same as another word)

Use the **first letter** of the word you are looking for to get to the right section of the dictionary, then the **second letter** to narrow down your search, and so on.

FACT FILE

Animal:	Rhino beetle
Habitat:	Poinciana trees and bush turkey nests
Weight:	Up to 85 g
Lifespan:	2 to 3 years
Diet:	Rotten wood and mulch

Task 1 Write the following groups of words in alphabetical order, in the blank columns.

S		B		W	
shell		bare		whether	
shelf		barn		whenever	
sheen		bark		whereabouts	
shed		barred		wherever	
sheep		barge		wheel	

Task 2   Use a dictionary to find out the definitions and the word type for the following.

	Definition	**Word type**
a threaten	_____	_____
b impressive	_____	_____
c species	_____	_____
d abdomen	_____	_____

Task 3   Use a dictionary or thesaurus to find synonyms for the following words.

a discover (verb)   _____

b poison (noun)   _____

c prey (verb)   _____

d important (adjective)   _____

e awful (adjective)   _____

WILD FACT
Rhino beetle males are very impressive, with horns that make them look like a small rhinoceros. They use these to fight with other males.

WILD FACT
Rhino beetles are not aggressive, but watch out for their sticky legs and the small claws at the end. If they feel threatened, they make a hissing noise by rubbing their wing covers against their abdomens.

Exploring Further ...

Which word from columns B, C or D would **not** be found between the words in column A? Write your answer in column E.

A	B	C	D	E
snake ... sugar	snip	spear	super	
beetle ... beside	beggar	bend	bean	
rhinoceros ... rope	robber	rose	rock	
camel ... caramel	castle	cape	candle	

Now charge your way to pages 44–45 to record what you have learned in your explorer's logbook.

Quick test

Now try these questions. Give yourself 1 mark for every correct answer – but only if you answer each part of the question correctly.

1   Add either the suffix tion or sion to these words to make nouns.

a except _____   b confuse _____

2   Add the prefix dis or mis to these words to give them a negative meaning.

a similar _____   b understanding _____

c guided _____   d content _____

3   Use the correct suffix to make nouns from these words.

a technic _____   b confess _____

4   Underline the silent letters in the words below.

a gnome   b knotted

c wrist   d hour

5   Unravel the anagrams to find words that end with que or gue.

a ealgue _____   b hecque _____

c aidgolue _____   d quitnae _____

6   Add either the prefix il or ir to give the following words a negative meaning.

a responsible _____   b logical _____

c rational _____   d legal _____

7   Put these words into alphabetical order: koala   kangaroo   kookaburra

_____

8   The words below have been spelt as they sound. Write the correct spelling on the line next to each one. Clue: they all have either an eigh, ei or ey spelling!

a wayt _____   b disobay _____

c bayge _____   d nay _____

9   Place an apostrophe to show possession after the following nouns in bold.

a Six **e x p l o r e r s** log books were lost in the outback.

b The **e x p e d i t i o n s** leader said we would make camp soon.

c One **s n a k e s** scaly skin was yellow, black and beige.

10 Put these words into alphabetical order: outwards   outback   outbound

_____

11 Circle the correct spelling of the underlined words.

She was given good advice/advise for recording outback animals.

At the end of the expedition, she past/passed with flying colours.

12 Put these words into alphabetical order:

desert   dessert   desperate

_____

13 Write a matching homophone for the following words.

a dear   _____   b hall   _____

14 Add the prefix un, im or in to these words to give them a negative meaning.

a happy   _____   b appropriate   _____

c prepared   _____   d possible   _____

15 These words have an 'i' sound in the middle but they have been spelt incorrectly. Write the correct spelling on the line next to each.

a eucaliptus   _____   b tipical   _____

16 Add the prefixes re, sub or inter to the following to make new words.

a marine   _____   b national   _____

c submit   _____   d apply   _____

e heading   _____   f galactic   _____

17 The following words end in either sure or ture but they have a letter missing. Complete the word by inserting the missing letter.

a adven _ ure   b trea _ ure

c pic _ ure   d plea _ ure

18 Change these nouns by using the suffix ous to make adjectives.

a curiosity   _____   b courtesy   _____

c courage   _____

19 Add the suffixes ing and ed to the following one-syllable words.

a bark   _____   _____

b trick   _____   _____

20 Turn these adjectives into adverbs by adding the suffix ly.

a happy   _____   b crazy   _____

How did you do?   1–5 Try again!   6–10 Good try!   /20

11–15 Great work!   16–20 Excellent exploring!

43

Explorer's Logbook

Tick off the topics as you complete them and then colour in the star.

How do you feel?
- Needs practice
- Nearly there
- Got it!

Prefixes dis and mis ☐

The suffix ly ☐

Silent letters ☐

Apostrophes for possession ☐

Suffixes beginning with a vowel ☐

Tricky spellings ☐

Prefixes un, in, im, ir and il ☐

Prefixes re, sub and inter ☐

Prefixes super, anti and auto ☐

Homophones and near-homophones ☐

Endings sounding like shun ☐

Words ending sure and ture ☐

Words with an ay sound ☐

Letter strings ou and ough ☐

k and sh sounds spelt ch ☐

The suffix ation ☐

g sound gue and k sound que ☐

Dictionary work ☐

Words with the s sound spelt sc ☐

Words ending ous ☐

Answers

Pages 2–3

Task 1

a parking, parked
b picking, picked
c tracking, tracked
d sorting, sorted

Task 2

	ing	ed
open	**opening**	**opened**
trumpet	**trumpeting**	**trumpeted**
fidget	**fidgeting**	**fidgeted**
limit	**limiting**	**limited**

Task 3

a forbidden
b committed
c occurred
d regretting

Exploring Further...

a itmad - admit, admitting, admitted
b wasren – answer, answering, answered
c premit – permit, permitting, permitted

Pages 4–5

Task 1

a formation
b consideration
c plantation
d confirmation
e confrontation

Task 2

a continuation
b exaggeration
c examination
d creation

Task 3

a fascination
b preparation
c temptation
d illustration
e exclamation

Exploring Further...

communicate	**communication**
transport	**transportation**
register	**registration**
locate	**location**

Pages 6–7

Task 1

Adjective	Adverb
calm	**calmly**
nice	**nicely**
sweet	**sweetly**
pleasant	**pleasantly**
brave	**bravely**

Task 2

a terribly
b simply
c basically
d frantically

Task 3

a happily
b lazily
c hungrily
d angrily

Exploring Further...

Adjective	Adverb	Sentence
enthusiastic	**enthusiastically**	Appropriate sentences containing the adverbs in column to the left.
comical	**comically**	
nimble	**nimbly**	

Pages 8–9

Task 1

a unhappy
b inaccurate
c unstable
d inactive
e indecent

Task 2

a irregular
b irrational
c incapable
d inoffensive
e irresponsible

Task 3

a il teriatel - illiterate
b imp sonreal - impersonal
c im morla - immoral
d il galel - illegal

Exploring Further...

inadequate, unnecessary, illegible, irresponsible

Pages 10–11

Task 1

a disappoint
b misunderstand
c dishonest
d disconnect
e misfortune

Task 2

a dissimilar
b disagree
c misheard
d disadvantage

Task 3

a Not faithful or loyal: disloyal
b Spell incorrectly: misspell
c Not honourable: dishonourable
d Not connected: disconnect/disjointed
e Bad luck: misfortune

Exploring Further...

R	A	N	C	D	B	X	N	D	E
D	A	L	W	W	Q	E	Y	I	V
A	I	E	W	A	K	F	D	S	A
E	U	V	P	A	C	I	E	C	H
L	P	T	T	P	S	Q	Y	O	E
S	H	S	S	T	A	W	D	V	B
I	I	I	R	G	U	S	A	E	S
M	U	U	Q	I	O	I	R	R	I
M	S	Y	E	B	O	S	I	D	M
T	M	M	I	S	P	L	A	C	E

Pages 12–13

Task 1

a reappear: appear again
b redecorate: decorate again
c rediscover: discover again
d redo: do again

Task 2

a subscribe — to arrange to receive something, e.g. a magazine
b subheading — a heading given to a section of writing
c subtitle — translation of foreign language on screen
d subway — an underground walkway

Task 3

a interchangeable
b Researchers
c resubmit
d intermingle

Exploring Further...

subheading, submerge, international, interact, resend, react, refresh

Pages 14–15

Task 1

a exceptional ability or powers
b a large shop with lots of variety
c a very famous and successful celebrity
d a very famous and successful model

Task 2

a antibiotic
b anticlockwise
c antisocial

Task 3

a autograph — your own signature
b autopilot — automatic steering device
c superstore — extra-large shop
d antibacterial — active against bacteria

Exploring Further...

a supernatural
b superwoman
c supersize
d superstore

Pages 16–17

Task 1

a nature
b researcher
c furniture

Task 2

a ruevent — venture
b ruseleap — pleasure
c rutereac — creature
d ruseclo en — enclosure
e triceups — pictures

Task 3

venture, creatures, pictures, enclosure, pleasure

Exploring Further...

Across
2 literature
6 future

Down
1 vulture
3 temperature
4 treasure
5 fracture

Pages 18–19

Task 1

Answers will vary. Accept any appropriate words starting with a silent letter.

Task 2

gnarl, comb, Wednesday, island, sword, honest

Task 3

a doubt
b knew
c wrack
d knowledge
e sign

Exploring Further...

g: design foreign gnome
b: crumb bomb thumb
n: autumn column hymn
t: fasten castle whistle

Pages 20–21

Task 1

a dangerous
b mountainous
c famous
d outrageous
e ridiculous
f envious

Task 2

a vigorous — strong and healthy
b glamorous — stylish and fashionable
c jealous — envious
d enormous — extremely large

Task 3

famous, various, poisonous, tremendous

Exploring Further...

S	N	X	S	S	C	D	S	Q	T	D	K
H	T	K	U	U	O	H	U	X	R	W	V
V	R	O	O	O	U	I	O	X	E	S	H
T	P	M	I	M	R	L	I	Y	M	U	Y
T	E	T	R	R	A	A	V	B	E	O	V
O	U	L	U	O	G	R	B	J	N	R	G
D	M	J	C	N	E	I	O	S	D	T	E
U	R	P	D	E	O	O	Z	U	O	S	X
W	V	R	S	T	U	U	Q	O	U	A	L
E	I	D	H	T	S	S	O	M	S	S	S
S	U	O	L	A	E	J	A	A	O	I	N
S	U	O	I	R	E	S	F	E	U	D	S

Pages 22–23

Task 1

a weight
b vein
c neighbour
d reign
e weird
f beige
g eighty
h heir

Task 2

a (ways/weighs)
b (They/thay)
c (neighbour/neybour)
d (ate/eight)
e (survay/survey)

Task 3

a prey
b beige
c sleigh
d disobey

Exploring Further...

a veils
b disobey
c weight
d beige

Pages 24–25

Task 1

a The crocodile's teeth.
b The pelican's feet.
c The bat's wing span.
d The camel's hump.
e The snake's venom.
f The kangaroo's pouch

Task 2

a kookaburras'
b dingoes'
c koalas'
d platypuses'

Task 3

a Chris's
b Australia's
c Cairns's

Exploring Further...

a My friend's map was found covered in muddy paw prints.
b All the explorers' sunhats were stolen by some cheeky koala bears.
c The small expedition's final camp was close to the billabongs.

Pages 26–27

Task 1

a write
b scene
c whether
d knot
e hear
f meat

Task 2
a The carpet snake kills by constricting its <u>prey</u>.
b The laughing kookaburra nests in <u>holes</u> in trees.
c My friend, <u>whose</u> dinner was eaten by a possum, was starving.

Task 3
Answers will vary. Accept any given sentences using each word in the correct context.

Exploring Further...
a wandered
b accept
c guest

Pages 28–29
Task 1
a ache
b school
c stomachs
d mechanic

Task 2
a character
b chemist
c chorus
d echo

Task 3
a parachute
b architect
c scheme
d anchor

Exploring Further...
a chef
b chauffeur
c machine
d moustache

An appropriate short story using the four words in context.

Pages 30–31
Task 1
a ascend — to move upwards
b crescent — curved, sickle-shaped
c disciple — a follower of a leader
d descend — to move downwards

Task 2
a disciples
b ascent
c crescent
d descended

Task 3
a fluorescent
b miscellaneous
c resuscitate
d scent
e adolescent
f descend

Exploring Further...
Answers will vary. Accept any given sentence using each word in the correct context.

Pages 32–33
Task 1
a analogue
b synagogue
c colleague
d league

Task 2
fatigue, tongues, dialogue, rogue

Task 3
Appropriate sentences using the words in the correct context

Exploring Further...

M	O	E	R	M	F	F	E	C	E
O	O	R	U	Z	G	U	O	L	U
N	J	P	C	G	Q	X	D	I	G
O	B	R	A	I	N	I	X	Q	I
L	O	C	T	Q	A	I	W	U	T
O	R	N	I	L	U	V	R	E	A
G	A	S	O	G	J	E	N	E	F
U	S	G	D	E	Y	Y	G	S	M
E	U	G	O	L	O	R	P	B	U
E	T	O	N	G	U	E	M	B	Z

Pages 34–35
Task 1
a countries
b double
c trouble

Task 2
a young
b cousin
c encourage
d couple

Task 3
a tough
b rough
c enough
d courage

Exploring Further...
Across
2 double
4 nourishment
6 courage

Down
1 country
3 touch
5 rough

Pages 36–37
Task 1
a symbol
b Egypt
c pyramid
d mystery
e hymn

Task 2
a cymbals
b syllable
c oxygen
d gym

Task 3
a additional
b original
c probable
d beetle
e ankle

Exploring Further...
a capital
b practical
c possible
d spectacle

Pages 38–39
Task 1
a action
b completion
c injection
d interruption
e coordination

Task 2
a expression
b comprehension
c tension
d permission

Task 3
a electrician
b magician
c musician
d optician

Exploring Further...
a politics — politician
b extend — extension
c possess — possession
d complete — completion

Pages 40–41
Task 1

S		B		W	
shell	**shed**	bare	**bare**	whether	**wheel**
shelf	**sheen**	barn	**barge**	whenever	**whenever**
sheen	**sheep**	bark	**bark**	whereabouts	**whereabouts**
shed	**shelf**	bared	**barn**	wherever	**wherever**
sheep	**shell**	barge	**barred**	wheel	**whether**

Task 2
a to endanger — verb
b magnificent — adjective
c a group of similar living organisms — noun
d stomach — noun

NB: definition answers may vary.